Do plants eat animals?

Contents

Written by Sally Morgan

Illustrated by Nuno Alexandre Vieira

Collins

What's in this book?

Listen and say.

jungle

trees

spider

Download the audio at www.collins.co.uk/839839

fly

plants

🎧 Sally and Daddy are looking at some plants.

"Why is this one closed, Daddy?" asked Sally.

"It's eating," said Daddy.

"What's it eating?" asked Sally.

"A fly," said Daddy.

"Do plants eat animals?" asked Sally.

"Some plants do," said Daddy.

Making food

Plants need the sun to make food.

Animals don't make food. Animals eat plants or meat.

A carnivore is an animal that eats meat.

Some plants are carnivores too. They eat small animals like spiders and flies.

Venus flytrap

This small plant is called a Venus flytrap. It is a carnivore.

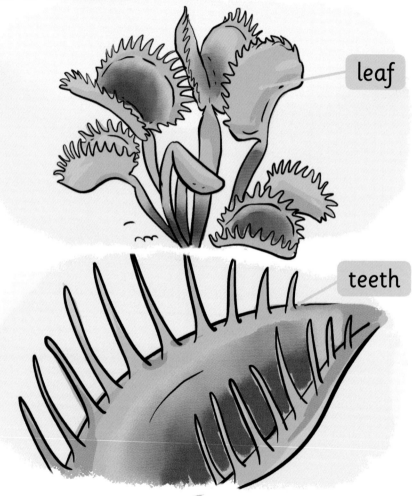

leaf

teeth

Its leaves are green and red. The leaf looks like a mouth with teeth.

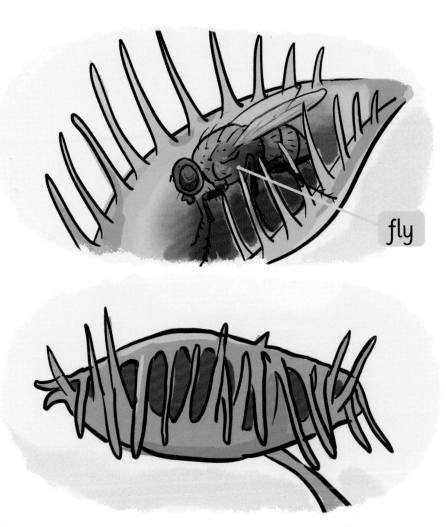

fly

Small animals see the red colour. The leaf closes when an animal touches the teeth. It's very quick!

The animal can't get away. Then the plant eats the animal.

Sundews

Sundews are small plants. They grow in wet places. They have long, sticky hairs. The hairs are like glue.

When a fly walks on the leaf, it can't move. Then the plant eats the fly.

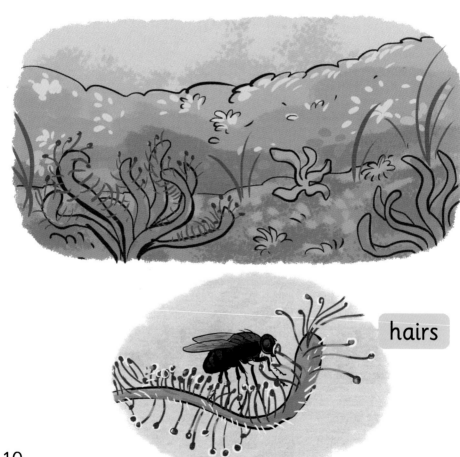

hairs

Sundews catch and eat bees, flies and spiders.

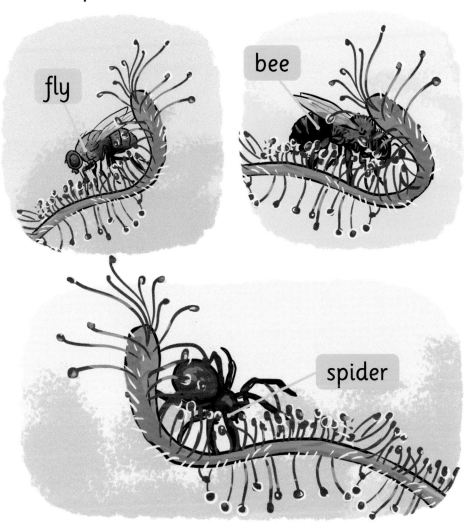

fly

bee

spider

Pitcher plants

Jungles are very hot and wet places.
Many tall trees, animals and plants live here.
Some of the plants eat small animals!

This is a pitcher plant. The leaves look like cups. The leaves hold water.

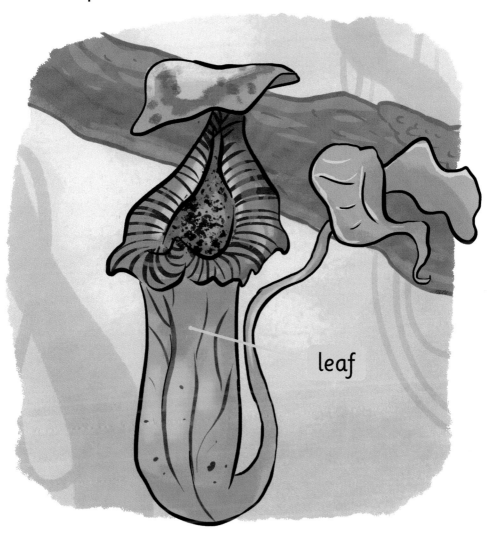

leaf

This pitcher plant is growing on a tree. Some pitcher plants live on the ground.

Different pitcher plants have different leaves.

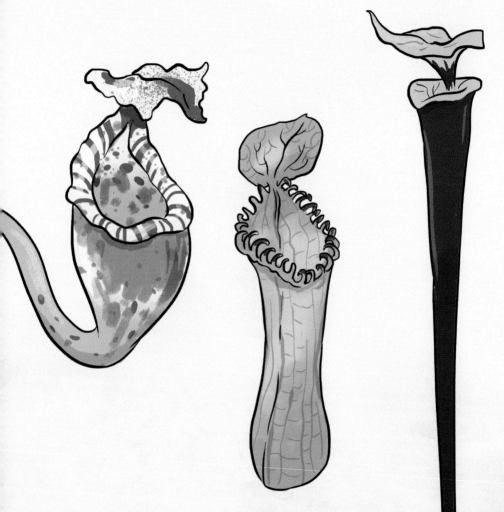

Some pitcher plants are tall and thin.
Some pitcher plants are short.

This pitcher plant looks like a bowl.

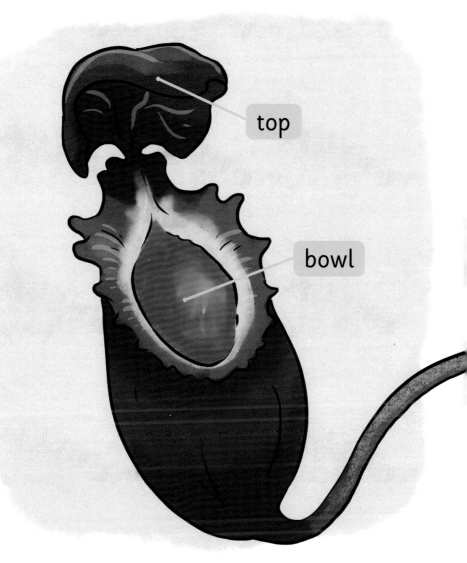

top

bowl

Its leaves are green and red. Its leaf has
two parts. It has a bowl and a top.

Pitcher plants smell nice.

Small animals think there is food. They go into the leaf and look for food.

smell

Then the animals fall into the water at the bottom. They can't get out.

Look in this pitcher plant. Can you see the spider in the water?

The waterwheel plant

These plants live in water.

This is a waterwheel plant. Its leaves look like wheels. The leaves have many small parts. Each part has a trap at the end.

The trap has lots of small hairs. When a very small water animal moves the hairs, the trap closes. The animal can't get out.

Grow a Venus flytrap at home

You can grow Venus flytrap plants in your home.

Put your Venus flytrap plant by a window.
Give it some water. You can give it flies!
Don't give it too many!

Picture dictionary

Listen and repeat

hairs

leaves

plant

sticky

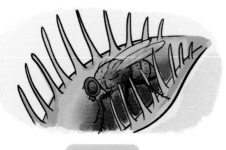

teeth

wheel

1 Look and match

pitcher plant

Venus flytrap

waterwheel plant

sundew plant

 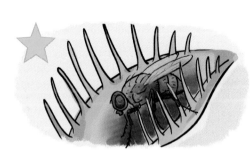

2 Listen and say

Collins

Published by Collins
An imprint of HarperCollins*Publishers*
Westerhill Road
Bishopbriggs
Glasgow
G64 2QT

HarperCollins *Publishers*
Macken House,
39/40 Mayor Street Upper,
Dublin 1
D01 C9W8
Ireland

William Collins' dream of knowledge for all began with the publication of his first book in 1819.

A self-educated mill worker, he not only enriched millions of lives, but also founded a flourishing publishing house. Today, staying true to this spirit, Collins books are packed with inspiration, innovation and practical expertise. They place you at the centre of a world of possibility and give you exactly what you need to explore it.

© HarperCollins*Publishers* Limited 2020

10 9 8 7 6 5 4 3

ISBN 978-0-00-839839-2

Collins® and COBUILD® are registered trademarks of HarperCollins*Publishers* Limited

www.collins.co.uk/elt

British Library Cataloguing in Publication Data

A catalogue record for this publication is available from the British Library.

Author: Sally Morgan
Illustrator: Nuno Alexandre Vieira (Beehive)
Series editor: Rebecca Adlard
Publishing manager: Lisa Todd
Product managers: Jennifer Hall and Caroline Green
In-house editor: Alma Puts Keren
Project manager: Emily Hooton
Editor: Barbara MacKay
Proofreaders: Natalie Murray and Michael Lamb
Cover designer: Kevin Robbins
Typesetter: 2Hoots Publishing Services Ltd
Audio produced by id audio, London
Reading guide author: Emma Wilkinson
Production controller: Rachel Weaver
Printed and bound in the UK by Pureprint

MIX
Paper | Supporting responsible forestry
FSC
www.fsc.org
FSC™ C007454

This book is produced from independently certified FSC™ paper to ensure responsible forest management.

For more information visit:
www.harpercollins.co.uk/green

Download the audio for this book and a reading guide for parents and teachers at www.collins.co.uk/839839